Pursuing
Integrity

DANIEL

New Community Bible Study Series

Old Testament

    Exodus: Journey toward God
    1 and 2 Samuel: Growing a Heart for God
    Nehemiah: Overcoming Challenges
    Psalms Vol. 1: Encountering God
    Psalms Vol. 2: Life-Changing Lessons
    Daniel: Pursuing Integrity

New Testament

    Sermon on the Mount 1: Connect with God
    Sermon on the Mount 2: Connect with Others
    The Lord's Prayer: Praying with Power
    Parables: Imagine Life God's Way
    Luke: Lessons from Jesus
    Acts: Build Community
    Romans: Find Freedom
    2 Corinthians: Serving from the Heart
    Philippians: Run the Race
    Colossians: Discover the New You
    James: Live Wisely
    1 Peter: Stand Strong
    1 John: Love Each Other
    Revelation: Experience God's Power

JOHN ORTBERG

WITH KEVIN & SHERRY HARNEY

New Community
KNOWING. LOVING. SERVING. CELEBRATING.

Pursuing
Integrity

DANIEL

ZONDERVAN.com/
AUTHORTRACKER
follow your favorite authors

ZONDERVAN°

Daniel: Pursuing Integrity
Copyright © 2008 by Willow Creek Association

Requests for information should be addressed to:

Zondervan, *Grand Rapids, Michigan* 49530

ISBN 978-0-310-28053-8

Interior design by Sherri Hoffman

Printed in the United States of America

QG 02-27-14

CONTENTS

G od has created us for community. This need is built into the very fiber of our being, the DNA of our spirit. As Christians, our deepest desire is to see the truth of God's Word as it influences our relationships with others. We long for a dynamic encounter with God's Word, intimate closeness with his people, and radical transformation of our lives. But how can we accomplish those three difficult tasks?

The New Community Bible Study Series creates a place for all of this to happen. In-depth Bible study, community-building opportunities, and life-changing applications are all built into every session of this small group study guide.

How to Build Community

How do we build a strong, healthy Christian community? The whole concept for this study grows out of a fundamental understanding of Christian community that is dynamic and transformational. We believe that Christians don't simply gather to exchange doctrinal affirmations. Rather, believers are called by God to get into each other's lives. We are family, for better or for worse, and we need to connect with each other.

Community is not built through sitting in the same building and singing the same songs. It is forged in the fires of life. When we know each other deeply — the good, the bad, and the ugly — community is experienced. Community grows when we learn to rejoice with one another, celebrating life. Roots grow deep when we know we are loved by others and are free to extend love to them as well. Finally, community deepens and is built when we commit to serve each other and let others serve us. This process of doing ministry and humbly receiving the ministry of others is critical for healthy community life.

Build Community Through Knowing and Being Known

We all long to know others deeply and to be fully known by them. Although we might run from this level of intimacy at times, we all want to have people in our lives who trust us enough to disclose the deep and tender parts of themselves. In turn, we want to reveal some of our feelings, expressing them freely to people we trust.

The first section of each of these six studies creates a place for deep knowing and being known. Through serious reflection on the truth of Scripture, you will be invited to communicate parts of your heart and life with your small group members. You might even discover yourself opening parts of your heart that you have thus far kept hidden. The Bible study and discussion questions do not encourage surface conversation. The only way to go deep in knowing others and being known by them is to dig deep, and this takes work. Knowing others also takes trust — that you will honor each other and respect each other's confidences.

Build Community Through Celebrating and Being Celebrated

If you have not had a good blush recently, read a short book in the Bible called Song of Songs. It's a record of a bride and groom writing poetic and romantic love letters to each other. They are freely celebrating every conceivable aspect of each other's personality, character, and physical appearance. At one point the groom says, "You have made my heart beat fast with a single glance from your eyes." Song of Songs is a reckless celebration of life, love, and all that is good.

We need to recapture the joy and freedom of celebration. In every session of this study, your group will commit to celebrate together. Although there are many ways to express joy, we will let our expression of celebration come through prayer. In each session you will take time to come before the God of joy and celebrate who he is and what he is doing. You will also have opportunity to celebrate what God is doing in your life and the lives of those who are a part of your small group. You will become a community of affirmation, celebration, and joy through your prayer time together.

You will need to be sensitive during this time of prayer together. Not everyone feels comfortable praying with a group of people. Be aware that each person is starting at a different place in their freedom to pray in a group, so be patient. Seek to promote a warm and welcoming atmosphere where each person can stretch a little and learn what it means to be a community that celebrates with God in the center.

Build Community Through Loving and Being Loved

Unless we are exchanging deeply committed levels of love with a few people, we will die slowly on the inside. This is precisely why so many people feel almost nothing at all. If we don't learn to exchange love with family and friends, we will eventually grow numb and no longer believe love is even a possibility. This is not God's plan. He hungers for us to be loved and to give love to others. As a matter of fact, he wants this for us even more than we want it for ourselves.

Every session in this study will address the area of loving and being loved. You will be challenged, in your personal life and as a small group, to be intentional and consistent about building loving relationships. You will get practical tools and be encouraged to set measurable goals for giving and receiving love.

Build Community Through Serving and Being Served

Community is about serving and humbly allowing others to serve you. The single most stirring example of this is recorded in John 13, where Jesus takes the position of the lowest servant and washes the feet of his followers. He gives them a powerful example and then calls them to follow. Servanthood is at the very core of community. To sustain deep relationships over a long period of time, there must be humility and a willingness to serve each other.

At the close of each session will be a clear challenge to servanthood. As a group, and as individual followers of Christ, you will discover that community is built through serving others. You will also find that your own small group members will grow in their ability to extend service to your life.

Bible Study Basics

To get the most out of this study, you will need to prepare and participate. Here are some guidelines to help you.

Preparing for the Study

1. If possible, even if you are not the leader, look over each session before you meet, read the Bible passages, and answer the questions. The more you are prepared, the more you will gain from the study.
2. Begin your preparation with prayer. Ask God to help you understand the passage and apply it to your life.
3. A good modern translation, such as the New International Version, Today's New International Version, the New American Standard Bible, or the New Revised Standard Version, will give you the most help. Questions in this guide are based on the New International Version.
4. Read and reread the passages. You must know what the passage says before you can understand what it means and how it applies to you.
5. Write your answers in the spaces provided in the study guide. This will help you participate more fully in the discussion and will also help you personalize what you are learning.
6. Keep a Bible dictionary handy to look up unfamiliar words, names, or places.

Participating in the Study

1. Be willing to join in the discussion. The leader of the group will not be lecturing but will encourage people to discuss what they have learned in the passage. Plan to share what God has taught you during your preparation time.
2. Stick to the passages being studied. Base your answers on the verses being discussed rather than on outside authorities such as commentaries or your favorite author or speaker.

3. Try to be sensitive to the other members of the group. Listen attentively when they speak, and be affirming whenever you can. This will encourage more hesistant members of the group to participate.
4. Be careful not to dominate the discussion. By all means participate, but allow others to have equal time.
5. If you are a discussion leader or a participant who wants further insights, you will find additional comments in the Leader's Notes at the back of the book.

Daniel:
Pursuing Integrity

Daniel was one of the brightest and best of Israel, born into a family of high social standing. He was physically attractive ... *GQ* cover material. He had a sharp mind and seemed to pick things up very naturally. He also had a high level of what some would call "emotional intelligence"—people smarts. On top of all of this, Daniel had an authentic faith that went far beyond head knowledge of religious facts to a heart that was fully devoted as a follower of Yahweh.

Daniel would have had all the dreams that young men with great potential have. In Judah the whole world was a wide open door right in front of him. He would have gone to a great school and received an excellent education. From there he would have been recruited into a top organization in his field of choice and gone on to glittering success. He would have married a nice girl, lived in an enviable home, raised a wonderful family, occupied a prominent place in the temple, and had a model life. He would have been on the fast track to do great things for God and for God's people.

But there were a few bumps on the road to paradise.

Life did not turn out the way Daniel planned. Nothing ended up as expected. Instead of becoming a poster boy among the people of Judah, Daniel became a prisoner of war. A king by the name of Nebuchadnezzar invaded the territory of Israel, and Jerusalem fell. The dreaded Babylonian army killed most of the men and took many women, children, and young men captive. Daniel was among those herded back to Babylon in a human caravan of sorrow.

Daniel's homeland had been bulldozed by a pagan army. Many of his family and friends would have died in battle or been executed. The temple of God in Jerusalem was desecrated and the sacred contents were shipped to Babylon and stored in the shrine of a pagan god. The hope of God's chosen people seemed to be crushed.

Daniel would come to adulthood and spend the rest of his life in a foreign land. Separated from cherished culture and relationships, he would have to learn and speak a strange language and serve an alien king. He would even lose his name and be assigned a new one. Stripped from him was his birth name ... a name with deep significance: "Daniel" meant "the Lord will judge." Thrust upon him was a new Babylonian name, "Belteshazzar," which Nebuchadnezzar states is a name "after the name of my god" (Daniel 4:8). Daniel started in Judah when everything looked promising. He ended up in Babylon, and it seemed like the bottom dropped out.

One of life's big questions is, "What will you do when the bottom drops out and you end up in Babylon?" For Daniel, we see that his years in Babylon became a laboratory that refined and defined him. He and his friends discovered that pursuing integrity and spiritual excellence rarely happens in a safe, comfortable place. Instead, God used a furnace, a lion's den, and a foreign country as places they would meet him and have life-changing experiences.

What will you do when you end up where you never expected? The truth is, all of us will have seasons when the address on the mailbox of our life simply reads: Babylon.

Babylon is where you find yourself when life does not turn out the way you planned:

> When a relationship becomes conflicted and looks like it is beyond restoration,
>
> When a marriage starts to skid sideways and love seems far away,
>
> When your greatest vocational hopes die,
>
> When somebody you trust wounds you deeply,
>
> When you realize that a deep prayer will never be answered the way you had hoped,
>
> When a loved one is terminally ill,
>
> When money runs out but the bills keep coming, or
>
> When your fears seem bigger than your faith.

You are in Babylon when you feel cut off from the life you wanted, dreamed of, and planned on. Like Daniel, you wonder if you will ever get home. Worst of all, you wonder if God even knows ... does he hear your cries for help? Or, has he forgotten his promise?

In these times of life God is still there. Like Daniel and his friends, if we hold fast to the God who loves us, we will discover that he still closes the mouths of lions, protects from the flames, delivers from mad kings, answers prayer, shows up in power, and grows the hearts of his children. Yes, in Babylon we discover that integrity and spiritual depth grow in the strangest of places and in the toughest of times.

Spiritual Resiliency

DANIEL I

There's a whole field in the social sciences that studies people who have experienced suffering or major crises, in an attempt to identify the consequences of such trauma on the human mind and spirit. Researchers have studied, among others, POWs from the Korean War and the Vietnam War as well as fifty-two hostages who were held fourteen months in Iran.

As you might expect, these studies showed that a lot of people became defeated by such difficult ordeals. Their spirit withered and they simply gave up. But the studies also made a surprising finding: many people don't just survive traumatic times; they actually seem to thrive and grow through them. For these people, trauma, loss, and pain actually enlarge their capacity to handle problems—they become stronger as a result. Researchers have come to call these folks "resilient" and the capacity to thrive in challenging and difficult situations "resiliency."

When we look at the life of Daniel, we see one of the most spiritually resilient persons in human history. Daniel lost virtually everything. But, through it all, he exuded a sense of strength, confidence, and hope in God. Such resiliency can be a model for each of us as we face the tough times of life.

Making the Connection

1. Tell about a person you know who has faced deep pain and loss in life but has displayed a resilient spirit.

Share a time you faced a difficult situation but felt the presence of God sustain you and grant resiliency as you walked through that season of your life.

Knowing and Being Known

Read Daniel 1:1 – 21

2. What were some of the losses, changes, and traumas that Daniel and his friends faced, and how could these experiences have deflated and discouraged them?

3. In the midst of this tragic time in Israel's history, how do you see God still present and at work among his people?

Spiritually Resilient People Resolve

Spiritually resilient people have a profound level of personal resolve to honor their deepest values. They refuse to live as passive victims of circumstances. They are determined that they will not get tangled up in things that might cause them to betray their deepest commitments. Ultimately, their resolve is to honor God no matter the price.

Daniel modeled this kind of resolve. If you read Daniel 1:1 –7 it appears that the Babylonians are in the driver's seat. Nebuchadnezzar determines to conquer Israel. He decides to cart off its most sacred objects and take the most gifted young people as prisoners of war. He enrolls these young POWs in his leadership academy and decides on the entrance criteria and subject matter. The dean of the school determines their names, their new identities, their menu. Daniel and his friends have no say, input, or influence on any of this.

The easiest thing in the world would have been for Daniel to feel like he was just a passive victim of forces way too big for him. But one characteristic of a spiritually resilient person is resolve, and Daniel was about to express this—even if it cost him big time! Verse 8 says, "But Daniel resolved not to defile himself with the royal food and wine, and he asked the chief official for permission not to defile himself this way." In the midst of all the determining and demanding of King Nebuchadnezzar, Daniel made a decision ... he resolved in his heart.

Read Daniel 1:1 – 10

4. Have you ever done something that was difficult, unpopular, or went against the grain of a cultural norm? Describe what happened.

How did your resolve impact you and the people around you?

5. Describe a situation in which you resolved to do something God-honoring, but discovered it was (or is) hard to live out the commitment.

How can your group members pray for you and encourage you to stand strong in this specific area of your life?

Spiritually Resilient People Respond

Daniel's resolve was solid in his heart. But resolve alone was not enough. He also had to respond ... he had to do something! So he went to the dean of the school to discuss the meal plan. Daniel was willing to accept the name change and the new clothes, and he was ready to learn a new language, but he resolved not to become "defiled" by eating the king's rich food.

We don't know exactly why Daniel refused to eat the food. It could have been related to the Jewish ceremonial laws about diet. Maybe the king's food had been offered to idols ... this was not uncommon in ancient times. Whatever the reason, Daniel knew he needed to draw a line, to take a stand. So he responded by presenting a specific course of action to those who oversaw his training, education, and diet. He showed great wisdom as he laid out a plan that would allow him and his friends to eat different food; he even gave a proposed timeline to confirm that the results would be agreeable to all the parties concerned. What an amazing example of an effective response that grew out of a firm resolve!

Read Daniel 1:11 – 17

6. Write down an area of your life in which you resolve to do something you truly believe will honor God:

Area of resolve: _____

_____

_____

Next, write down two responses (actions) that will be required if you are going to live out this resolve:

Response: _____

_____

_____

Response: _____

_____

_____

7. Describe your area of resolve and your responses to others in the group.

What are some things that could get in the way of you living out this resolve, and how might you prepare for these roadblocks?

Spiritually Resilient People Relate

Spiritually resilient people are committed to living in community. They recognize that having others around them for support, encouragement, and accountability can mean the difference between life and death. For Daniel, he found this network in a small group he formed with three friends: Hananiah, Mishael, and Azariah. In a strange land, they had a safe haven in each other.

Julius Segal, a gifted researcher in the area of resiliency, tells a story about a man who experienced this need for community at a staggering level. Vice Admiral James Stockdale served 2,714 days as a POW in Vietnam. Through these years he experienced isolation, pain, and torment like most of us can't begin to imagine. On one occasion his captors shackled him in glaring sunshine for three blistering days while guards beat him to keep him from sleeping. After being beaten, Stockdale heard a towel snapping out a secret message in a code the POWs had devised. Four simple but unforgettable letters ... G.B.U.S. Jim's fellow POWs were saying to him: "God bless you, Stockdale." Julius Segal explains that for these men, the briefest experiences of community, of being connected, offered lifesaving hope.

8. What is one relational network you have built and nurtured that helps you remain healthy and resilient in the journey of life?

9. How might group members offer a growing level of support to each other?

Spiritually Resilient People Remember

Spiritually resilient people are careful to remember that their life, and even their suffering, has meaning and purpose in the eyes of God. Researchers say that one of the factors which causes people to give up is believing their suffering has no meaning or purpose. Many times it is not the intensity of the suffering that crushes the spirit; it's the meaninglessness of it.

For Daniel and his friends, the key was to remember that God was still on the throne working through all of the circumstances, even when things looked hopeless. They needed to remember that God had a plan for them and their nation. As they remembered these truths, they could endure the painful loss and challenges of being strangers in a strange land.

10. Tell about a time when God's grace and presence helped you though a difficult situation or life experience.

How does remembering God's help in the past strengthen you for the future?

11. The Bible consistently calls us to pass on stories of God's faithfulness to the next generations—our children and grandchildren. If you grew up with an older person in your life who told you stories of faith (from the Bible and their

own life experiences), how did this person help shape your understanding of God's presence and power?

Name a younger person God has placed in your life and describe how you can be more intentional about sharing stories of faith with this person.

Celebrating and Being Celebrated

Read the following Bible passage and then lift up prayers of thanks and celebration for those who have passed on the faith to you: parents, grandparents, aunts and uncles, pastors, Sunday school teachers, or anyone who shared stories of faith and inspired you to walk with Jesus.

> What we have heard and known,
> what our fathers have told us.
> We will not hide them from their children;
> we will tell the next generation
> the praiseworthy deeds of the LORD,
> his power, and the wonders he has done.
> He decreed statutes for Jacob
> and established the law in Israel,
> which he commanded our forefathers
> to teach their children,
> so the next generation would know them,
> even the children yet to be born,
> and they in turn would tell their children.

Then they would put their trust in God
and would not forget his deeds
but would keep his commands. (Psalm 78:3–7)

Loving and Being Loved

Your small group serves as a place where you can relate and connect with other followers of Jesus. By gathering together to study the Bible, pray, and learn we create space for friendship to be forged and love to grow. In addition to your formal group sessions, consider scheduling a time to go out to dinner, see a play, spend an afternoon at a park, or engage in some other group activity. Let this informal time become yet another opportunity to grow deeper friendships with other group members.

Serving and Being Served

The story of Vice Admiral James Stockdale is a vivid example of how community, even the encouragement of a message sent with snapping towels, can offer hope in a dark moment. As a group, identify a person in your church or community who is facing a time of ongoing struggle and pain. Then decide on a practical, tangible way your group can "snap out" a message of love and blessing to this person.

Let God Be God

DANIEL 2

Some years ago a man named Ernest Kurtz wrote what's become the definitive history of the Alcoholics Anonymous movement, a book entitled *Not-God*. In it he contended that the alcoholics' basic problem is their refusal to acknowledge limitation and weakness. They tend to live under the delusion that they are in control of everything, when the truth is, they can't even control themselves. "Fundamental to the recovery process," he wrote, "is that healing and sanity begin with a single realization that *I am not God.*"

This "I am God" illusion is not limited to alcoholics. Behind the very first sin ever committed was this same deceptive illusion. According to Genesis 3:5 the serpent said to the woman, "God knows that when you eat of it [the fruit], your eyes will be opened, and you will be like God, knowing good and evil." It was the first temptation. "You'll be master of your own universe. You don't have to bend the knee. You don't have to submit to somebody else's wisdom. You can get away with flouting the moral law of the universe. You will be like God."

People have been falling for that same line since the beginning of time.

Making the Connection

1. What possible indicators might be present in a person who is living with an "I am God" attitude?

Knowing and Being Known

The "I Am God" Syndrome

Nebuchadnezzar, the king of Babylon, saw the world as revolving around him. That often happens when everyone around you boldly declares, "The world revolves around you!" In ancient times, many kings claimed that they were God, and who was going to argue with them? Head of a powerful nation with a mighty army, Nebuchadnezzar was in control; people existed to make him happy; all the pleasures of this world were at his fingertips. He was fully caught up in the "I am God" syndrome.

Many people today still live under this delusion. They may not be king or queen of a mighty nation, but they live as if the entire cosmos moves around them. Their guiding attitude in life is that their needs, desires, and dreams are what matters most. When mental health professionals evaluate people who have really run hard and far with this kind of attitude they use terms like "messianic complex" and "grandiosity." Put simply, when we get swept into a mind-set that says, "I am the center of the universe," we are experiencing the "I am God" syndrome.

Read Daniel 2:1 – 13

2. What are some signs that Nebuchadnezzar was caught up in the "I am God" syndrome?

3. The "I am God" syndrome can come in many shapes; it can be a minor case or a major outbreak. But when this sickness gets into our soul, it tends to impact every aspect of our life.

When the "I am God" sickness starts to grow in your heart, how does it show up in *one* of these areas:
- Your workplace and career

- Your marriage

- Your parenting

- Your friendships

- Your finances

- Your spiritual life

- Another area of your life: _____

Read Daniel 2:14 – 28

NG

GAVE credit to G

WENT TO COMPANIONS

I Am Not God

When Lyndon B. Johnson was president, he once asked Bill Moyers, his press secretary and also an ordained Southern Baptist minister, to pray at a cabinet meeting. As Moyers was praying (somewhat quietly) at the other end of the table, Johnson interrupted: "Speak up, Moyers, I can't hear you." To which Bill Moyers simply responded, "I wasn't talking to you, sir."

No matter how high we might climb on the ladder of this world, we will never be God. When we accept this reality, a fresh humility and perspective overflows in our heart, mind, and life. Everything changes!

NO ONE CAN INTERPRET DREAM, XG

4. Name three key indicators that show Daniel was profoundly aware he was not God.

-

-

-

How might we develop these same attitudes and actions as we seek to live a life that humbly declares we are not God?

5. When Daniel faced this life-threatening moment, he immediately went to a small cluster of friends and asked them to begin praying. Why is it essential for every follower of Jesus to have people in their life who can come alongside in prayer during challenging times?

What are some of the steps we can take to create a personal prayer support network?

6. When God revealed the interpretation of King Nebuchadnezzar's dream to Daniel, Daniel was adamant that God
alone deserved the credit and honor. Such an attitude is
characteristic of an "I am not God" life. Discuss situations in
which we are tempted to take credit and receive praise even
though God is the one who deserves it.

*What can we do to make a point of giving God the glory and
praise in these moments?*

You Are Not God ... But He Would Love to Meet You!

Daniel had a deep desire for Nebuchadnezzar to understand the spiritual reality that was unfolding right under his nose. Daniel knew God, and
he wanted the king to meet his Maker ... in a good way! At its heart, the
book of Daniel is about evangelism. Going into exile in a foreign country
looked like the end of the world for Daniel and his friends. Instead, God
used the situation as the evangelistic opportunity of a lifetime.

When we humbly declare, "I am not God," and "I am lost apart from
God," our whole outlook on life changes. Not only do we celebrate
God's saving grace, but we want others to experience it too. We devote
ourselves to doing whatever it takes to help people see God's presence
and power in this world. We take all kinds of risks, pay all kinds of prices,
and devote ourselves to helping other people meet the one true God.

Read Daniel 2:29–49

7. How did Daniel show courage and boldness in his testimony to Nebuchadnezzar?

G is one in Control

How did he show tact and gentleness?

Not about N, but about G

8. Do you know someone who needs a relationship with the rock-solid God of the universe? Write the person's name here.

How can your group pray for you as you seek to boldly and gently share God's love with this person?

The Freedom of Living an "I Am Not God" Life

If God is God and I am not, I can stop worrying.

When worry comes along we can allow it to be a prompting of the Holy Spirit to remind us that we don't carry the world on our shoulders. We can humbly say, "God, I'm going to give this situation to you. I lay my fears at your feet. I trust you to carry me through. You are God. I am not!"

Daniel was in a foreign land, under a death threat from an angry king, and profoundly aware that he did not have any personal power to exercise in this situation. Yet, he had an unquenchable certainty that his life was in the hands of a competent God. Subsequently, he didn't live in fear. He was not paralyzed by anxiety. He did not let worry rule his world.

9. Honestly assess the level of worry in your life and mark where you see yourself on the scale below:

1	2	3	4	5	6	7	8	9	10

I almost never worry	I worry occasionally	I worry all the time

Why did you rate yourself as you did?

10. What situation are you facing that could raise the level of worry and anxiety in your life?

If you were to focus on the spiritual reality that you are not God, and trust him to be in control, how might this lower your worry quotient?

11. One of the biggest antidotes for worry is prayer. Daniel modeled this in his life. The apostle Paul also taught this truth when he wrote these words:

> Do not be anxious about anything, but in everything, by prayer and petition, with thanksgiving, present your requests to God. And the peace of God, which transcends all understanding, will guard your hearts and your minds in Christ Jesus. (Philippians 4:6–7)

How have you experienced the peace-bringing power of prayer in times that could have been anxiety filled?

Celebrating and Being Celebrated

Even when we're unsure of the outcome, we can learn to praise God in the middle of our stories. That is what Daniel did. Right in the midst of this situation with King Nebuchadnezzar's dream, he stopped to praise God:

> Then Daniel praised the God of heaven and said:
> "Praise be to the name of God for ever and ever;
>   wisdom and power are his.

He changes times and seasons;
    he sets up kings and deposes them.
He gives wisdom to the wise
    and knowledge to the discerning.
He reveals deep and hidden things;
    he knows what lies in darkness,
    and light dwells with him.
I thank and praise you, O God of my fathers:
    You have given me wisdom and power,
you have made known to me what we asked of you,
    you have made known to us the dream of the king."
(Daniel 2:19–23)

Whatever lies just head for us—good times or hard times—we know God holds the world in his hands and can confidently trust in his care. Like Daniel, we can gather together with a small group of friends, right in the middle of our stories, and pour out our hearts in worship and adoration. Celebrate who God is and what he is doing, right in the middle of your story.

Loving and Being Loved

Because prayer is a powerful antidote to worry, one of the best things you can do for each other is offer honest, powerful, Spirit-anointed prayers. Ask God to lift worry, crush anxiety, bring confidence, and reveal his presence in the lives of your group members. In questions 9 and 10 you discussed some of the worries your group members are facing. Take time to pray for each other and ask for God's peace to replace worry.

Serving and Being Served

Some of life's worry comes from very real challenges and needs we face. As you listened to group members share some of their anxiety-causing situations, consider adding some action to your prayers for them. Keep praying, but also do something in the coming weeks to help lift the specific burden they shared with the group.

Meeting God in the Furnace

DANIEL 3

Some years ago, due to an unexplained explosion, 118 crewmen in a Russian submarine tragically died. Twenty-three of these men survived in an isolated chamber for several hours after the explosion. What would have gone through your mind had you been in this submarine, deep below the ocean, knowing there was little chance of rescue?

One of the sailors, twenty-seven-year-old Dimitri Kolesnikov, wrote a note while he waited to die, which was later displayed in a black frame next to the coffin at his funeral service. On it were two words: "Mustn't despair." It's not real clear for whom the note was written. It may be that he was telling himself to keep hoping against hope that somebody would come to their rescue. More likely, he wrote these words for his wife, as a message of hope to carry her forward after his death.

A *Time* magazine essay once explored what people do when they know they are drawing near the end of life. It's almost an instinctive response to send a message to someone. That's what many passengers on a JAL airliner did as they spiraled to their death in 1985. Similarly, Jewish survivors in a 1940s Warsaw ghetto, having seen all their friends shot or starve to death, took their last moments to write letters, which they hid in crevices in a wall in hopes that somebody would read them and remember their story.

In that final moment, all the scaffolding of life gets stripped away. All the toys we spent a lifetime collecting and protecting seem worthless. All the efforts to increase our success, reputation, security, wealth, comfort, and ease seem hollow. In a moment like this a person is left with what they really believe. Everything else melts away.

Making the Connection

1. If you knew you had a few minutes left to live, what would you write to your loved ones? (For those who want to volunteer, take time to read your reflections to your group members.)

Live life to its fullest

What would you want them to gain from what you wrote?

Peace, Contentment

Knowing and Being Known

Furnace Avoidance

A moment came in the lives of three young men in ancient Babylon that was quite similar to what Dimitri Kolesnikov faced. They knew the end of their life was very near. The one big difference: they could have avoided it. All they had to do was cooperate and play along with the king's request. These were young men of great promise. They had risen to positions of eminence in the world's most powerful nation. They could look forward to great families, deeply fulfilling lives, doing noble things for their people and for their God. Their hearts were full of hopes and dreams. They had a lot to live for.

For these three men—Shadrach, Meshach, and Abednego—death was eminently escapable. All they had to do was say the word, bend the knee, and their nightmare would be over. They would live and be restored to positions of power, honor, and status. Instead, they were headed toward unimaginable pain and death. They could have avoided the furnace, but they chose to face it instead.

Christians living in a world as comfortable as what many of us inhabit can be tempted to believe that God would never want us to struggle or face a furnace. In fact, our primary goal in life can become what might be called "furnace avoidance." We can find ourselves praying, "God, deliver me from pain, discomfort, suffering, and inconvenience. Make my life smooth. Make my journey easy. Make my years on this earth comfortable. Remove all obstacles from my path."

Read Daniel 3:1 – 18

2. What did Shadrach, Meshach, and Abednego have to do if they were going to avoid the furnace?

   Kneel + worship n'a idol.

   What were some of the spiritual implications if they had practiced furnace avoidance at this critical moment of their lives?

   They would have broken one of the 10 Commandments

3. What are some of the church's current theological systems and teachings that tell us that furnace avoidance is exactly what we *should* practice? ?

   Church doesn't teach this

4. Where might these teachings lead us if we follow them to their logical conclusion?

5. No one likes the furnace times of life. What are some of the normal and natural reasons we tend to avoid discomfort, suffering, and pain?

Read Daniel 3:19 – 25

Meeting God in the Furnace

Shadrach, Meshach, and Abednego became members of a very exclusive club. The membership requirements were simple: walk through the furnace and stay alive. But there was a fourth member of the furnace club. This member appeared after the other three were thrown in and ended up being their deliverer. It's an amazing picture: these three young men walking around in the roaring inferno, chatting with a fourth figure in the flames. A small group meeting right there in the furnace!

Who was this fourth man who appeared from nowhere, looked like a son of the gods, and cheated death? Well, the text doesn't say, but I think it was Jesus. It sounds like the kind of thing he would do.

I wonder what they said to each other. I wonder if the fourth man in the furnace told them how proud the Father was of their loyalty and love. I wonder if he told them that because of this one act of faithfulness, their names would be remembered for thousands of years; that for centuries men and women who faced suffering, persecution, trial, or even death would be immeasurably strengthened by hearing their story.

I wonder what they said to the fourth man. I'll bet they poured out adoration, gratitude, and wonder like never before. It's a funny thing; they came to this place with a fearless resolve to withhold worship from a false god. They ended up worshiping the one true God. The furnace looked like the end of their lives but it turned out to be the greatest thing they would ever experience. It is where they met God!

6. Describe a time you went through an experience of pain, suffering, or loss and how God came and walked with you through this furnace.

   When I lost loved ones, God eased the pain by letting me know they were in a better place

7. How has your faith grown deeper over the years through furnace times?

   I've always gotten thru tough times

8. What is a furnace time you are facing right now (or that you see on the horizon)?

   Potential loss of relatives + friends

   How can your group members pray for you as you go through this challenging season?

   Not here yet

Lessons from the Furnace

Though going into the furnace seemed to be the last thing Shadrach, Meshach, and Abednego wanted to do, it turned out to be the defining event of their lives. Ironically, that which looked like a certain death sentence turned out to be the safest place of all. Why? Because God was there. The truth is, sometimes God delivers people *from* the furnace, but sometimes he delivers people *in* the furnace.

Full devotion to Jesus can lead to places that look scary, dangerous, and painful. In the end, it turns out that Jesus meets us in these places. Jesus said, "Whoever wants to be my disciple must deny themselves and take up their cross and follow me. For whoever wants to save their life will lose it, but whoever loses their life for me will find it" (Matthew 16:24–25 TNIV). When we walk with Jesus, we carry a cross, walk through furnaces, lay down our lives—and he is with us every step of the way.

Read Daniel 3:24–30

9. How did the furnace experience of Shadrach, Meshach, and Abednego shape their future and the future of their people?

They were promoted + became famoly for themself of years

10. How did the bold faithfulness of these three men impact Nebuchadnezzar and the nation of Babylon?

They became believers in God

11. Tell about how God used one of your furnace experiences to bear witness to the presence, power, and grace of Jesus.

Celebrating and Being Celebrated

God loves to meet people in the furnace. If God had a calendar on his wall and we could turn back the pages, we would see many appointments through the years. Meet Corrie ten Boom. Meet Martin Luther King Jr. Meet Dietrich Bonhoeffer. Meet Mother Teresa. Then, as you turned the calendar pages, you would find your name. You would see time after time when God has met you in the furnace and walked with you. As a group, thank God in prayer for the times he has met you in the furnace.

Loving and Being Loved

God spends lots of time in furnaces; he has felt the heat. In the ultimate furnace, he went to the cross and bore the weight of human sin for us. As an act of sacrificial love, consider doing something dangerous. Make a decision to stop asking for less heat and flames in your life. Don't ask for an easier, richer, more pleasant, or more secure life. Instead, tell Jesus you want to go with him wherever he goes. Commit to walking with him as he leads . . . even if this means stepping into the furnace.

Serving and Being Served

There are easy service assignments and there are furnace service assignments. Pray about committing to an act of service that will stretch you. Go on a trip to a part of the world where there is real suffering and let your heart be broken as God's heart is broken. Mentor a person who is in jail. Give away something you really love, something that will hurt, and offer this money to the poor and the broken. Pray about some way you can get into serving in a context that will stretch your faith and cause you to meet God in the furnace.

It's Hard to Be Humble

DANIEL 4

God opposes pride and loves humility. According to Daniel 4:37, King Nebuchadnezzar learned this lesson the hard way.

> Now I, Nebuchadnezzar, praise and exalt and glorify the King of heaven, because everything he does is right and all his ways are just. And those who walk in pride he is able to humble.

This same message of God's desire for people to flee pride and walk in humility is echoed throughout the pages of the Bible. Consider these verses:

> Whoever slanders his neighbor in secret,
>   him will I put to silence;
> whoever has haughty eyes and a proud heart,
>   him will I not endure. (Psalm 101:5)

> The LORD detests all the proud of heart.
>   Be sure of this: They will not go unpunished.
>   (Proverbs 16:5)

> But he gives us more grace. That is why Scripture says: "God opposes the proud but gives grace to the humble." (James 4:6)

Why does God make such a big deal about pride? Because our world doesn't! And sadly, neither does the church.

In my years as a pastor, many people have confided their struggles to me, but I have yet to have somebody ask for an appointment to talk about their pride problems. Go to the self-help section in any bookstore. See how many books you find about overcoming pride and developing humility. The problem is, most people don't see pride as a sin.

A church leader many centuries ago named Gregory the Great wrote, "Pride makes me think that I am the cause of my achievements, and that I deserve my abilities. Pride leads me to despise other people that don't measure up. Pride causes an illusion of self-sufficiency."

An item once printed in *Reader's Digest* somewhat humorously captures the idea. A woman was so tired of always being corrected by her husband that she decided the next time it happened, she would be ready with the perfect comeback. When the moment finally came and he corrected her yet again, she responded, "You know, even a broken clock is right once a day!" To which he replied, "Twice a day."

In our world, pride is looked upon as irritating at worst and maybe even a virtue by some. God *always* sees it as a problem.

Making the Connection

1. What are some of the signs that our society, and even the church, can have an accepting attitude toward pride?

Rarely hear people give God the credit for their accomplishments

Knowing and Being Known

Reason for Pride

If anyone ever had reason to be proud and impressed with their accomplishments, it was King Nebuchadnezzar. Babylon, the capital of his empire, was the site of so much building under Nebuchadnezzar's direction that it took 126 pages just to record the inscriptions carved into the buildings that he had constructed. He could have been interviewed on "Good Morning Babylon" to share the secrets of a successful life. He could have written self-help books like *Seven Practices of Pleased and Prosperous Palace People.*

Nebuchadnezzar's achievements were astounding in the scope of human history. You've heard of the seven wonders of the ancient world. Maybe the most impressive was the Hanging Gardens of Babylon, thought to have been constructed by Nebuchadnezzar for a wife who missed her mountainous homeland. From the roof of his palace, Nebuchadnezzar could see a double wall running all the way around his city. One ancient historian says the outer wall was 56 miles long, and so wide that you could turn a four-horse chariot around on it There was simply no city like it anywhere.

Read Daniel 4:4 – 18

2. What are some of the reasons people can feel self-secure, overconfident, and prideful in our world today?

They don't see pride as a problem

3. When pride begins to creep into your heart and life, what is it that drives and grows this attitude?

Turning away from God

We All Need a Daniel

Daniel gave King Nebuchadnezzar an amazing gift. He spoke the truth. Knowing it could cost him his position of influence, or even his life, Daniel was still willing to tell Nebuchadnezzar about the potential disaster headed his way if he refused to humble his heart and resist the lure of pride. We all need someone in our lives who will tell us the truth ... in a way that puts things into honest perspective.

There is a wonderful little story about how our outlook can be altered when the truth is spoken. On a road trip with his wife, the CEO of a huge corporation pulls their car into a service station for a fill-up. When he returns from paying for the gas, he notices his wife engaged in an animated conversation with a service station attendant. It turns out that his wife had dated the attendant years ago when they were in high school. After a moment of silence as they resume their trip, the CEO smugly says to his wife, "I'll bet I know what you're thinking. You're pretty lucky that you married me, the CEO of a big corporation, and not a service station attendant." His wife says, "No, actually I was thinking if I had married him and not you, he'd be the CEO of a great corporation, and you'd be a service station attendant."

Read Daniel 4:19–27

4. Name someone in your life who has a "Daniel" role of speaking the truth to you. How has God used this person to make you a stronger, more devoted follower of Christ?

5. Why is it so difficult to speak the truth to others when we see pride and sin growing in their lives?

We should straighten out our lives first,

Why is it important to press through these reasons and commit to be a Daniel to those we love?

Plan A and Plan B

God's plan A for Nebuchadnezzar and for each of us is simple ... humble yourself. If we follow his plan, flee from pride, give him glory, and renounce our sinful ways, grace flows!

God's plan B for Nebuchadnezzar and for us is much more painful. If we refuse to humble ourselves, God is perfectly able and willing to humble us. If we persist in prideful and arrogant rebellion, God can bring us down from our "high place."

A quick survey of the Bible reveals numerous examples of people who refused to cooperate by taking plan A. In each case, God instituted plan B. Think about Jonah. God said, "Go and preach repentance to the people of Nineveh." Jonah said, "No!" And, after an epic storm and a famous fish ride, Jonah ended up in Nineveh anyway. God spoke to Pharaoh through Moses and said, "Let my people go." Pharaoh pridefully said, "No." But after gnats, frogs, hail, and worse, the people of Israel were sent away with gifts. The apostle Paul persecuted Christians and resisted God until he was knocked to the ground, was blinded, and finally repented.

God would prefer each of us choose plan A, but if we refuse, we must remember that God is very capable of instituting plan B. By the way, plan A is always better!

Read Daniel 4:28 – 34

6. What consequences did Nebuchadnezzar face because he refused to humble himself and ended up taking the plan B route?

Driven from men
ate grass like oxen
body wet
hair like eagle feathers
nails like birds claws

If Nebuchadnezzar could visit your small group today and give a personal exhortation about taking plan A over plan B, what do you think he would say?

humble yourself
give up your pride
don't rebel

7. There are many areas of life in which God wants us to humble our hearts, repent, and receive his grace. When we refuse, or when we keep delaying our repentance week after week and month after month, God will often lovingly intervene and begin a process of humbling us. Take a moment on your own to reflect on the following questions:

  • What is one area of my life in which I am aware God wants me to humble myself before him by repenting and changing my ways?

  • If I refuse to humble myself and make the changes I know will honor God, what are some consequences I might face?

  • If God decides to institute a plan B in this area of my life, what might happen?

  • What steps could I take today to humble myself in this area of my life?

- Who could pray for me and keep me accountable to take specific steps to humble myself in this part of my life?

If you feel comfortable doing so, tell your group members about the area of life in which you believe God wants you to humble yourself and one step you will be taking to do this.

Blessed Interruptions

Nebuchadnezzar was going to have his perfect life, successful career, and legacy as king interrupted by a prolonged bout with insanity. Everything would be put on hold as God pushed a divine pause button on Nebuchadnezzar's story to break his pride and teach him humility. It seemed like a painful process, but it was a dramatic act of love, a blessed interruption.

Sometimes God places those he loves under the "spiritual discipline of being interrupted." A very interesting connection exists between our response to interruptions and the presence of humility or pride in our lives. Dietrich Bonhoeffer writes about humility in service to each other in his book, *Life Together.* He says, "In Christian community, one service we should perform for each other is that of active helpfulness. This means simple assistance in trifling matters. There is a multitude of these things wherever people live. Nobody is too good for the humblest service.... One who worries about the loss of time, that such petty outward acts of helpfulness entail, is usually taking the importance of his own career too solemnly. God will be constantly crossing our paths and canceling our plans by sending us people with claims and requests. We must be ready to allow ourselves to be interrupted by God."

8. How do a person's responses to daily interruptions act as indicators of their levels of pride and humility?

What responses show that a person is humble and what responses show a prideful heart?

9. What are some of the daily interruptions God typically sends your way and how do you tend to respond to them?

How could you respond with a more humble spirit the next time one of these interruptions presents itself?

The Hope of Humility

When Nebuchadnezzar finally hit bottom, he looked up and his sanity was restored. And when that happened, his immediate response was to praise God. What a striking picture. He didn't say, "I can't believe all the years I've wasted; I'll never recover from this humiliation and embarrassment." No, he responded with adoration. A whole season of his life had slipped by (many scholars think about seven years), yet he showed not regret but thankfulness. His pride broken, his heart humble ... Nebuchadnezzar was free, a new man.

10. Daniel 4 begins and ends with sections of praise from the lips of Nebuchadnezzar. Verses 2 – 3 set the stage for the story that follows. Verses 34 – 37 recount what happened after his plan B journey. What did Nebuchadnezzar learn about God through his experiences captured in this chapter?

11. In the times of life when you have chosen to humble yourself, or when God has lovingly humbled you, what have you learned about God?

How have you seen humility lead to hope?

Celebrating and Being Celebrated

Ask a designated person to read the sections of praise and adoration from Daniel 4 below and on page 49. Or read them in unison as a group, if you all feel comfortable doing this.

It is my pleasure to tell you about the miraculous signs and wonders that the Most High God has performed for me.

How great are his signs,
  how mighty his wonders!
His kingdom is an eternal kingdom;
  his dominion endures from generation to generation.
  (vv. 2–3)

His dominion is an eternal dominion;
  his kingdom endures from generation to generation.
All the peoples of the earth
  are regarded as nothing.
He does as he pleases
  with the powers of heaven
  and the peoples of the earth.
No one can hold back his hand
  or say to him: "What have you done?" (vv. 34–35)

As a group lift up prayers of praise for God's love, power, and commitment to help us grow in humility.

Loving and Being Loved

The man behind the counter at the mini-mart looked like he was in his early seventies. He couldn't speak English very well. I was just buying a newspaper and was in a hurry. Apparently he had just started working there and couldn't figure out how to get the code entered into the register. While he fumbled with my simple transaction, my reflexive thoughts were, *This is taking too much time. Why should I have to wait like this? Why should I be delayed?* I showed my impatience with my body language ... it was no secret that I was a bit irritated.

Not until sometime later did I stop to really think about the man at the store. It struck me that he was at an age when a lot of people want to retire, but here he was having to learn a new job, not to mention a new language and a new culture. On top of it all, he had to take care of an impatient customer ... me! I was humbled as I realized (after the fact) that this is somebody God loves and sent his Son to die for.

In the next week, when you find yourself feeling irritable, impatient, or interrupted, stop and remember that every person you lock eyes with is loved by God. Pray for eyes to see them the way God does. Then, seek to show the love of Jesus in how you respond in each situation.

Serving and Being Served

One of the most unforgettable stories Jesus ever told was a story about an interruption. Two religious leaders, real spiritual guys, come across someone who lay beaten, bleeding, and in need of help but decide to ignore him. Only a foreigner, a guy on the fringe, stops to respond with true care and compassion. Read Luke 10:30–37 during the next week. Then spend time praying that God will help you see the broken people who are along the road as you travel through life. Ask the Holy Spirit to give you power and compassion to help those in need.

The Cost of Character

DANIEL 6

For many years publishers have produced children's Bible story-books that have occasionally misrepresented the heartbeat of the biblical stories. There is no indication that this has been malicious or intentional, of course; it is merely a sad by-product of trying to make complex human drama and the divine mystery of God understandable to seven-year-olds.

When we take a children's storybook approach to the Bible we can actually think that Samson and Delilah was a love story, or sing cheerful songs about the "Arky, arky" and miss the tragedy of God's judgment in the flood. It is this same simple perspective that frames the story of Daniel in the lions' den as primarily about him sleeping peacefully among some big, cute, and furry felines.

Yes, Daniel was put in a lions' den. Yes, the lions were kept from gobbling him up for dinner. Yes, this was an amazing miracle! But there is so much more to the story.

Daniel 6 teaches us about how living with a high level of integrity and character can cost more than we dream. It reveals that habits of faith and a life of faithfulness are not private matters, but should be lived in the public eye. This chapter also portrays the power of a fearless witness. When God's people hold fast to their convictions, a watching world stands amazed. Of course, the whole lions' den part is very cool ... but it is time that we hear the rest of the story!

Making the Connection

1. If you grew up hearing Bible stories, what was one of your favorites and why did you like it?

   Noah & the flood, so different from my environment?

Many people who grew up hearing children's Bible stories later read the actual story in the Bible and are shocked that it is a very different version. If this has happened to you, share how you perceived a specific story as a child and how reading the biblical text as an adult put a whole new spin on the message.

Didn't realize there were so many bad folks + so few good ones.

Knowing and Being Known

Read Daniel 6:1 – 28

2. What do you learn about Daniel's character, lifestyle, and faith as you read this chapter?

He had much of god

3. What do you learn about the character and faith of Darius?

A Life of Exemplary Character

We live in a day and age when political leaders can look into a camera with a straight face and declare that their policies are what really matter and their personal character should not be an issue for their constituents.

TV and movie stars seem to bounce from jail to rehab to late-night parties to court appearances that look more like red-carpet events than legal proceedings intended to determine if they can keep custody of their own children. Sports figures emphatically defend their innocence, but blood tests keep showing the presence of performance-enhancing drugs.

More than any time in history there seems to be a famine of character. We need examples of people who say what they believe and then live it out. Character is about holding convictions that honor God and letting those deep beliefs shape all we say and do ... even when no one is watching! True character is about staying true to what we believe even when there are consequences.

Read Daniel 6:1 – 9

4. In this passage, the political leaders first tried to find a flaw in Daniel's character. What did their research turn up?

No flaws

When attacking Daniel's character did not work, how did they use the strength of his character against him?

They knew he would pray to God thereby breaking the King's future edict

5. Note some of the cultural trends and norms that can keep us from living with godly character.

6. Describe someone you have known who exemplifies consistent, godly character in every aspect of their life.

How has their example inspired you?

Unyielding Devotion to God

Daniel loved God. His faith was real and deep. By the time we catch up with him in chapter 6, he has been a political exile in Babylon for about sixty-five years! No longer a young man refusing to eat rich food from Nebuchadnezzar's table, he is now well into his seventies or older. Daniel has developed life disciplines and practices that grow out of a heart that is connected to his God, so three times a day he gets on his knees to pray. You can almost hear his old joints cracking as he lowers his elderly frame to the ground. His window is always open as he faces toward Jerusalem, the childhood home he has dreamed about for almost seven decades. This is his habit ... and everybody knows it!

Read Daniel 6:10 – 15

7. Name some disciplines or habits of faith that help you express your love and devotion to Jesus.

Prayer Church

8. What is a spiritual discipline you have wanted to develop, but it seems difficult to get it going, or keep it going, in your life?

How might your small group become a place of prayer, encouragement, and accountability that would propel you forward in developing this discipline of devotion?

The Power of a Witness

Daniel's willingness to die for what he believed became a witness to Darius and the world. It is interesting to note that the word "witness" comes from the root word *martyria*, from which we get the word "martyr." It literally means "a person who shows Christ's passion in life and death."

Throughout history many Christians have held to their faith in the face of persecution and have paid the ultimate price. Here are a few prayers lifted up by these faithful servants before they died:

Let me be steadfast in my faith to the end.
I have no hope of seeing my brethren again in this life.
If they kill me, let me die as a witness to my faith;
If I live, let me go on proclaiming it.
    Gabra Michael, died in 1855 in chains refusing to deny Jesus

Now at last I am beginning to be a disciple.
No earthly pleasure can bring me any good,
    no kingdom of this world.

It is better for me to perish and obtain Jesus Christ
    than to rule over the ends of the earth.
Let me win through to the light; that done I shall be complete.
Let me suffer as my Lord suffered.
    Ignatius of Antioch, killed by wild beasts in 107 AD

This is the end, but for me it is the beginning of life.
    Dietrich Bonhoeffer, executed in a Nazi death camp

Read Daniel 6:16 – 28

9. How did Daniel's witness, through actions and words, impact Darius?

10. Daniel was trapped by a deceitful plan hatched by work colleagues, other administrators whom he had surpassed in authority. (By the way, their plan backfired with ironic severity.) Describe ways people today might suffer persecution or personal attacks if they hold to their Christian faith without compromise.

    • In a home that does not embrace the Christian faith

    • In the workplace

    • On a school campus

    • In a community setting

    • In some other area of life: _____

11. What steps can a follower of Jesus take to stand strong and be a witness in times of persecution and pressure?

Celebrating and Being Celebrated

Sometime this week write a note to a person in your life who has exemplified godly character. Think about one or two ways their character has been a shining light in this dark world and let them know how these specific qualities have inspired you. Thank them for being a person of character.

Loving and Being Loved

As a group pray for courage to stand strong in your faith no matter what you face. If any group member is facing a specific time of pressure, persecution, or opposition, pray for them to stand strong and be a courageous witness for Jesus.

Serving and Being Served

A deceitful myth is being propagated in the church today. It goes like this: Far too many Christ followers are being overly forceful and aggressive with their faith. We are scaring people off. We are too enthusiastic. We need to settle down. It's time to back off.

This is a myth!

For every overly zealous and pushy Christian who needs to settle down a bit, there are thousands who should be challenged to be more engaged, intentional, prayerful, and active about sharing their faith. One of the best ways we can serve our world is through developing a winsome, consistent witness.

Consider serving your church (and community) by working in its outreach program. If your church does not already offer an outreach training experience on a regular basis, perhaps you can help get one started. All sorts of great resources are available, but three solid ones you might want to investigate are: *Becoming a Contagious Christian* (both the book and curriculum), by Mark Mittelberg, Lee Strobel, and Bill Hybels; *Reaching Out: Sharing God's Love Naturally*, by Bill Hybels; and *Just Walk Across the Room* (book and curriculum), also by Bill Hybels.

Dreams and Visions

DANIEL 7:1–14

Human beings are incurable predictors. There's something inside of all of us that can't resist forecasting the future. We predict the weather based on everything from extremely sophisticated radar to a groundhog. Every year sportswriters predict who is going to win the World Series and Super Bowl. Financial experts predict what will happen to the stock market and countless people hang their hopes on the advice.

When I was a little kid, folk knowledge said that you could predict the initials of the person you would marry by twisting off the stem of an apple while reciting the alphabet. Whatever letter the stem broke on was the initial of the person you were going to marry. People just seem to have an unstoppable hunger to know the future.

The book of Daniel traces a story that begins with a young man exiled to a foreign land, who decades later still holds to his character and convictions and ends up in a lions' den. In the years in between, we learn of pagan kings who encounter God and youth who defy royalty at the risk of their lives. Indeed, the first six chapters of Daniel are narrative stories that we can read and understand without complex interpretation.

But in chapter 7 things change dramatically as we enter into a kind of literature called apocalyptic. Filled with symbols, numbers, animals, angels, visions, and other vivid images, this same kind of literature can be found in Ezekiel and Revelation as well as other books of the Bible. In fact, it was a common style of writing and communication in the ancient world, often used when pointing to the future and speaking most powerfully to people living in times of great persecution. When we read these portions of the Bible, it is important to remember that such images made much more sense to people in the ancient world than they do to us today.

Making the Connection

1. Why do you think people spend so much time trying to predict the future?

   What kind of problems might arise when Christians work too hard at predicting the future, using the Bible to support their theory of how history will end?

   It may not happen + you'll lose credibility

Knowing and Being Known

Read Daniel 7:1 – 14

2. Though much of the imagery in this portion of Daniel is hard to understand, there is clarity on at least two terms. The "Ancient of Days" is a picture of God, while the term "Son of Man" is one Jesus used of himself in the New Testament. What do we learn about the "Ancient of Days" in this passage?

What do we learn about the "Son of Man" from this vision?

Be Ready for Conflict and Serious Problems

Throughout history, God's people have faced times of suffering. In many ways, persecution and struggle have been more common to followers of Christ than times of peace and ease. The imagery of the four beasts in Daniel 7 points to the reality that God's people should be ready for conflict and problems. They convey the destructiveness of human power when it is used in defiance of God's will.

One beast looks like a bear with three ribs in its mouth. This is a picture of violence and aggression. Violence leads to more violence. Hatred leads to more hatred. Killing leads to more killing. Look at a newspaper almost any day and then look at your own heart. Evil breeds and is never satisfied.

Another beast has four wings to show the swiftness with which evil can act. Yet another beast has ten horns because horns were an image of power. And ten of them on a single beast meant extraordinary power. The images of these beasts remind us that there are forces in this world that are hostile to God. There always have been, there are today, and there always will be. Therefore, the people of God can expect opposition, danger, suffering, and persecution. And when it comes, we are not to be surprised. We are to be prepared!

3. When you open the newspaper, turn on the TV, or look around your community and world, how do you know that lions, bears, leopards, and other powerful forces of evil are still at work?

4. In what specific ways do you see these forces working against God's will in *one* of the following arenas?

- The world of politics
- The news media
- The entertainment industry
- The educational system
- The religious systems of the world
- Some other arena: _____

5. How can awareness of these points of attack help followers of Christ stand strong against them?

Don't Give Up!

Many Christ followers today have a very safe and comfortable lifestyle. We are not thrown in jail or tortured for worshiping God. Most of us are not living in desperate poverty or fear of famine or illness. The truth is that such peace and security for Christians is an anomaly in the scope of church history.

We are tempted to think that if we face a serious problem with our health or finances, a job or a relationship, that somehow God has abandoned us. We have forgotten that we are in a war. It is not primarily a war about physical suffering, though it can be. It is primarily a spiritual conflict intended to pry men and women away from God. Daniel uses such vivid images to keep these truths in the forefront of our minds: We are in a war. Expect serious problems. Don't be surprised. Don't give up.

Read Daniel 7:9–14

6. If we live each day aware that we are in the midst of a spiritual battlefield, how might this change our expectations about how life should go?

7. What life experiences can discourage you and cause you to wonder if God is really in control of the universe?

What helps you hold to your faith in these times and stand strong for Jesus even when the battle rages around you?

God Is on the Throne!

The drama that unfolds in Daniel 7 begins by looking at the evil and turmoil that exist on this earth (vv. 1–8). But then the vision changes dramatically and our focus is turned upward, toward heaven (vv. 9–14). If we are going to face the evil in this world and keep from giving up, we need to see God! When we are captured by the glory of the Ancient of Days and the wonder of the Son of Man, hope fills our hearts, no matter what we might face.

In Daniel's vision we see that God is just, pure, and powerful. Each truth helps carry us through the good and bad times of life. When the Ancient of Days sits on the throne, we can be sure that he will make all things right. Injustice will be banished and justice will flow across the earth. As we gaze upon God and see his clothing as white as snow, we are captured by his dazzling purity, contrasted by the impurity of the world and our own hearts. This gives us hope that we can become pure as we walk with him. In the flames, fire, and blazing wheels, we see the power of the Ancient of Days. When we feel powerless, we are assured that he offers a reservoir of resources that has no end. God is on the throne. His justice will prevail, his purity will refine us, and his power is made available to all who follow him.

8. Think about the situation of Daniel and his fellow Israelites, still prisoners of war in a foreign land. How would the vision of the Ancient of Days seated on the throne have inspired them?

What was the contrast between the political and human situation they saw with their eyes and the spiritual reality God revealed in this vision?

9. When we encounter God on his throne ruling in power, we see each of life's challenges through new eyes. Consider God's attributes from Daniel's vision:

    • God is just ... he will bring justice into the unjust situations of this world.
    • God is holy ... he will purify that which is polluted by sin.
    • God is powerful ... he will sustain the weak and broken.

    Which of these attributes do you need most and how do you want to experience the Ancient of Days releasing this reality in your life?

God Wins

As we read Daniel 7, the tension mounts: powerful and evil beasts ... lions and bears and leopards, razor-sharp teeth of iron, horns, boastful words. The battle is on. The war is raging. Then we read:

> I kept looking until the beast was slain and its body destroyed and thrown into the blazing fire. (The other beasts had been stripped of their authority, but were allowed to live for a period of time.) (Daniel 7:11b–12)

It suddenly becomes clear: The Ancient of Days and the Son of Man have all authority and sovereign power. Their dominion and kingdom will never pass away. Simply put, God wins! What comfort this brings in times of persecution, struggle, and turmoil. We know how the story ends.

Read Daniel 7:11 – 14

10. Some people would never read the end of a book first ... it would ruin the experience. But when it comes to this life, reading the final chapter is the best thing we can do. When we know how the story ends, we get new perspective on the chapter we are living today. God will win and overcome all evil. As a matter of fact, through Jesus he has already won the final battle with sin, death, and the devil. How should this impact *one* of the following?

- How we face temptation
- How we deal with persecution
- Our desire to share God's love with others
- The way we serve and care for others
- The way we pray
- Some other area of our lives: _____

Celebrating and Being Celebrated

Using Daniel 7:9–14 as your guide, meditate on the truths revealed about God and then lift up group prayers of adoration, trust, hope, and celebration.

Loving and Being Loved

One way we show our love for God is by growing in purity. In Christ we are cleansed, but we are also called to continue growing in holiness. Take time on your own this week to ask a few of the questions below. Use them to stir you into prayer and actions that lead to holiness:

> Is there anything in your life that needs to be purified?
> Have you been involved in any financial practices that could dishonor God?
> Are you being tenacious about truth-telling or do you allow deceit in your words and life?
> Are you engaging in an area of sexual compromise?
> Do you have a cynical spirit?
> Do you struggle with gossip or a sharp and hurtful tongue?
> Do you have a judgmental spirit toward others?
> Is there any area of hidden sin that God wants to clean up?

As you reflect on these questions, invite the Holy Spirit to speak, convict, and bring power for change. Seek purity that will honor God and bring lasting joy to your life.

Serving and Being Served

We all encounter people who are discouraged and seem to be on the verge of giving up. If you know someone who is feeling this way, share Daniel 7:9–14 with them. Call them on the phone, write them a note or email, or drop by their home. Give them a vision of the One who is on the throne. Remind them that God wins. Then pray for them. Ask the Ancient of Days to open their eyes to see that he is in control, no matter what their eyes might see.

Session One – Spiritual Resiliency
DANIEL 1

Question 1

God is calling us to be like Daniel: to make a resolution in our hearts that will demand courage, wisdom, and spiritual resiliency. This is essential if we are going to survive and thrive in Babylon ... because the reality is that *all* of us will spend time in Babylon.

So many people say, "I want to get to know God better," or "I want to live with authentic joy," or "I want to build into the life of another person," or "I want to seize life by the throat and experience it to the fullest!" But instead of taking action on these hopes and dreams, they make excuses. "If only I weren't so busy." "If only things in my life were not so difficult." "If only other people had not done things to hurt or frustrate me." If we are going to experience consistent growth and become spiritually resilient, we will need to stop making excuses, resolve to walk with God no matter what we face, and get on with the journey.

Question 3

Daniel discovered something in Babylon that he might not have learned if he'd lived his whole life in Israel as he had planned. He discovered that Somebody was at work in Babylon before he got there and at every moment of his captivity. There is another key character in this story besides Daniel, his friends, and Nebuchadnezzar. Sometimes this key player gets missed in the flow of the story. Read Daniel 1:9, 17.

Questions 4–5

The writer of Daniel highlights the issue of resolve all through chapter 1 in a very colorful way. Though it is difficult to pick up in most translations, the same verb gets repeated three times. A literal rendering of verse 7 would be, "The chief of staff *deter-*

mined new names for them. He *determined* on Belteshazzar for Daniel and so on ..." Then verse 8: "But Daniel *determined* not to defile himself with rich food." In the first two instances, it's a Babylonian doing the determining, but the third time it's Daniel doing the determining. It could be translated, "Daniel resolved in his heart that he would honor God. He would not defile himself." He just decides ... he purposes in his heart.

It is difficult for modern readers to imagine how much courage this took on Daniel's part. Nebuchadnezzar was not the kind of leader who cut people a lot of slack. In 2 Kings 25:1–7, a puppet king named Zedekiah rebelled against him. Nebuchadnezzar captured Zedekiah and his family and had his sons killed before Zedekiah's eyes. Then Nebuchadnezzar had Zedekiah's eyes gouged out. He did this so that the last picture Zedekiah would carry in his mind for the rest of his life would be the execution of his sons.

If Nebuchadnezzar was comfortable slaughtering a man's children in front of his own eyes, imagine how he might respond to a young prisoner of war questioning his orders. You've heard of leaders with hands-on and hands-off management styles: Nebuchadnezzar had a "heads-off" management style. Knowing this makes the words of Daniel's supervisor all the more serious. He claims that if Daniel and the other youths look less healthy, it could cost him his head. He really meant it.

With all this background in mind, Daniel determines something. He does not view himself as the helpless pawn of circumstances beyond his control. Filled with magnificent courage and initiative and guided by wisdom, he chooses to honor God despite potentially dire consequences. Spiritually resilient people are that way. They resolve that they will honor God come what may.

Questions 6–7

It was not enough for Daniel to simply resolve this in his heart. He had to move into action. He goes to the dean of the school and makes his request. And the dean says, "But if I say yes to you, you'll end up looking weak and lack energy. And the king will have my head." That's his answer.

It is here we start to see Daniel's persistence and street smarts. Daniel says to himself, "Well, that's not exactly a yes, but it's not exactly a no." He goes to the guard the next level down the organizational chart and proposes an experiment: "Let's try this diet for ten days, and then you be the judge." Daniel exercises amazing initiative, courage, and faith that God will work. And God does!

Daniel goes to the head of the class; he becomes valedictorian. He and his friends are elevated. But note that this happens only because he resolved in his heart he would not get tangled up with anything that would betray his deepest values.

Each of us should regularly ask ourselves, "What do I need to resolve in my heart?" Do we need to end a relationship that dishonors God? Do we need to repent of unethical business practices? Do we need to seek first the kingdom of God by reordering our time? Is there an area of our lives in which we need to pursue healing, but we haven't done so because we've seen ourselves as victims? First, we must resolve in our hearts, then get ready to take action. If the Holy Spirit calls us to such a resolve, then we must seek his power to respond in a way that will honor God and lead to life transformation.

Questions 8–9

Daniel and his friends have become their own small group. They would go through school together. They surely studied and prayed and faced decisions together. Three of them would one day face the furnace together. They would one day help rule together. This one small group of devoted believers would change the course of a nation.

When you live in Babylon, you will not survive and thrive outside community. In times of struggle and persecution we are drawn to community, hunger for it, and do all we can to build it. But when things seem to be going fine, we can forget our need for it.

Community, deep friendship, spiritual intimacy: these things do not come easy. We have to fight for them. We need to make them part of our lifestyle. If someone is struggling with some difficult problem it is fair to ask, "Are you in community? Do you have a small group of trusted Christian brothers and sisters who support you, help you, pray for you, and give you wisdom?" If they tell you that they are not connected with community, encourage them to take intentional steps to get into a small group or find a source of regular connection with other Christ followers.

Questions 10–11

Who's the character that keeps getting mentioned in Daniel 1? It's God. The writer is convinced that God is at work right from the start; he knows what many of the Israelites did not know: that even Judah's defeat and the loss of the temple were not just random and meaningless events.

God was not asleep. God had not broken his promise or forgotten his dream. God was up to something in Babylon ... in the place of great suffering. God, as it turns out, loved even Babylon. God, as it turns out, even cared about Nebuchadnezzar. Whatever we suffer, we must remember: God is there with us.

Session Two – Let God Be God
DANIEL 2

Question 1

The heart of sin and spiritual confusion often begins with the tempting words, "You'll be like God." When we believe this lie, we start down a road of spiritual deception that spirals into the multifaceted depths of the "I am God" syndrome.

Alcoholics Anonymous recovery meetings always start with a reminder of spiritual sanity. The first words people utter are, "My name is _____. I'm an alcoholic." What they are saying is, "Just to be clear about who I am, I'm *not* God."

It's amazing how confused we get over this one single principle. Someone once made a simple but profound declaration, "The biggest difference between you and God is God doesn't think he's you." Failure to understand that we are not God can destroy our spiritual lives.

Questions 2–3

According to Daniel 2:1, this is the second year of Nebuchadnezzar's reign. Assyria, which had been Babylon's chief enemy, had completely collapsed five years earlier. Nebuchadnezzar is the absolute dictator of an empire that reigned with unchallenged authority over the known world.

Nebuchadnezzar had youth, strength, wealth, fame, and unparalleled power. The most secure person on the face of the earth, he is seen as a god by his people. But he's a god who can't sleep. A year into having everything he's always wanted, he discovers that everything is all wrong ... and he's troubled.

People who live under an "I am God" delusion are always just one bad dream — just one bad night's sleep away — from utter insecurity. They are building a house on sand, and it takes only one big storm to cause everything to come tumbling down.

Questions 4–6

Daniel's actions offered a crystal-clear demonstration that he was not God. For one thing, he *cried out for God's help*, acknowledging his own need. He was so vulnerable that he needed others to pray for and with him. What a great reminder that we are not in control of the universe ... the simple act of prayer. Then, Daniel *lifted up praise*. He admitted that God was the One who revealed things that were deep and hidden ... not Daniel! To top it off, Daniel *gave public credit to God*. He would not let people say, "Wow! Look what Daniel did." Instead, he made sure the king, and everyone else, knew that God alone deserved praise for this great revelation.

As we seek to live lives based on the truth that God is God and we are not, all three of these patterns should mark our lives. Every time we pray, we admit that we need God's leading, wisdom, and power to make it through the day. When we praise God, we express to him that he deserves the glory ... not us. And each time we see God do something wonderful and publicly give him the credit, we avoid the "I am God" syndrome.

Questions 7–8

Daniel had many reasons to shrink back, not least of which was that he could be killed. But he used exquisite wisdom and unquenchable boldness. First offering a simple, honest testimony of God's presence and power, he then revealed Nebuchadnezzar's dream and interpretation and made sure to give God the credit. The king's response was dramatic:

Then King Nebuchadnezzar fell prostrate before Daniel and paid him honor and ordered that an offering and incense be presented to him. The king said to Daniel, "Surely your God is the God of gods and the Lord of kings and a revealer of mysteries, for you were able to reveal this mystery." (Daniel 2:46–47)

Was Nebuchadnezzar converted at this point? Not likely. He's still engaged in pagan idolatry and oppressive violence. But Daniel doesn't give up on him, because he knows the God of heaven is at work even in Nebuchadnezzar's heart. His story is still being written.

Most people's spiritual journeys are usually not straight up the ladder. Often it's two steps forward and one step back. When we live with a deep awareness that God cares about people, we do all we can to introduce them to the God who already loves them. Like Daniel, we take risks, speak truth, give testimony, and trust that God is at work.

One other subtle theme that runs through this portion of Daniel's story is the way he always included his friends. He gathered them when the challenge arose so they could pray with and for him. When it came time to interpret the dream for the king, Daniel said, "*We'll* interpret the dream." He wanted his friends in on the credit. This is why, at the very end of the story, after the king has honored Daniel, he also elevated and honored Daniel's three friends.

Session Three — Meeting God in the Furnace
DANIEL 3

Questions 2–5

All Shadrach, Meshach, and Abednego had to do was fall down and worship the image … bow the knee. But they would not do it. They knew that God could deliver them, but even if he did not, they were not going to bow down. Life or death hung in the balance and they chose the furnace over compromise. That kind of devotion to God is rare in any generation.

The Bible is full of examples of such tenacious faithfulness to God. The apostle Paul faced all kinds of suffering just because he followed Jesus (see 2 Corinthians 11:23–29). He understood that this was part of the journey and was willing to embrace weakness and find the strength of God's presence rather than practice "furnace avoidance."

Today plenty of preachers and teachers, many of them on TV, try to convince their listeners that furnace avoidance is actually God's promise to the faithful. According to them, if we follow Jesus and walk in faith, we will never struggle, be sick, lack financial resources, or experience any pain in this life. A loving God would never ask his children to experience hardship, they say; instead, it's his job to bless us, make us rich, and protect us from even the smallest flame of the furnace.

The problem is that these people are wrong. God does not promise protection from any and all furnace experiences. What he *does* guarantee is that he will be with us no matter what we face. Sometimes God wants us to look to him in our weakness, accept his strength, and walk with him hand-in-hand through the flames.

Some people in your workplace may be far from God and exhibit behaviors that are quite painful for you. It might feel natural to pray, "God, get me out of here," to seek a transfer or a new job. But maybe God's plan is to keep you right where you are, at least today, so that he can use you. If this is God's will, know that you are not alone. This could end up being the best place in the world.

Maybe your furnace involves a messy relationship, a financial hardship, or a big sacrifice God wants you to make. In our day and age the common idol or golden statue we bow down to are things like "comfort," "ease," "security," and "success." It might be time for you to accept the power and presence of God as you hang in there instead of running away.

Questions 6–8

Stop for a moment and try to imagine the experience of these three young men during those final moments before they were thrown into the flames. They had resisted temptation, not bowed down, been faithful to the very end. And now they were going to die for their commitment to God.

Now picture them in the fire waiting for the searing pain and numbness, for the smoke inhalation that will suffocate them. But none of it comes. They don't feel any different. It begins to dawn on them that they're not even warm or tied up anymore. They're walking around in the furnace, a stroll through the flames. Then they do a head count. Shadrach ... one! Meshach ... two! Abednego ... three! All present and accounted for. Hey ... who is the fourth guy?

At the same time, the king also sees an extra man in the fire. We don't know for certain, but I believe it's Jesus, walking through the fire with the three men. It is a divine encounter, one they never could have experienced had they not been willing to go into the furnace.

Questions 10–11

In verse 21 the writer goes into some detail about the clothes that Shadrach, Meshach, and Abednego wore: the robes, trousers, turbans, and other garments. Why does he do this? He wants us to understand the extent of this miracle. Not only are the men saved, but God even protects their clothes. In fact, the clothes listed are so obscure that they are called by different names in different Bible translations. I think the term translated "robe" may be a covering for the upper body that had an inscription in Aramaic: "The king threw me in the fiery furnace and all I got was this lousy T-shirt!"

A key lesson from this encounter is the powerful witness to God's greatness. Nebuchadnezzar ends up praising God, even commending the three men for defying his commands and giving them big promotions. This is not normal kingly behavior! Some of his best soldiers had died in the flames because of his carelessness, and it did not even seem to register with him. He remains a hard-hearted guy, yet without doubt he's starting to change inside.

And what became of Shadrach, Meshach, and Abednego? We don't know. This is the last snapshot we have of them, the last time they're ever mentioned in Scripture. But I imagine they often reminisced about this great adventure, especially meeting the fourth man in the furnace.

Session Four — It's Hard to Be Humble
DANIEL 4

Question 1

I've seen people receive church discipline for sexual sin, financial wrongdoings, and scandals of all sorts. I cannot remember anyone receiving church discipline for a proud spirit or an arrogant attitude. God calls these things sin, but the church seems to give people a pass on them.

Sometimes pride is especially ingrained in those men and women who are considered spiritual giants and members of church leadership. That was true in Jesus' day. The scribes, Pharisees, and teachers of the Law were so renowned for a prideful attitude that it had come to be accepted as part of their high status as religious professionals.

But make no mistake: God detests pride, opposes it, and will pay it back in full. Pride is lethal to our relationship with him and with each other. This is why God calls us to humility and will do what it takes to drive pride out of our lives.

Questions 2–3

Hundreds of triggers can start us down the road of pride, among them success, wealth, beauty, and other things our world applauds. There are also spiritual triggers, such as a position in the church, a disciplined life, great biblical knowledge, and a devoted prayer life. It is interesting how we can become proud of the strangest things. Even a very humble person can begin to take pride in their humility!

Questions 4–5

This is a strange dream. At the center of it is a great tree—the tree of glory, which expresses the reality of Nebuchadnezzar's life. The tree is visible to the whole earth: everybody looks up to the king. This tree provides food for all, giving shelter to the beasts of the field and a nesting place to the birds: everybody depends on the king.

Nebuchadnezzar lives with constant reminders of how important he is—"You have become great and strong; your greatness has grown until it reaches the sky, and your dominion extends to distant parts of the earth" (Daniel 4:22). This is a man who understands power—how to acquire it, how to protect it, how to use it to further his agenda. The dream is a picture of proud and stubborn self-sufficiency. There is no acknowledgment of Nebuchadnezzar's dependence on God, no sense that one day he will be accountable to God as a steward and a servant to this great city.

Daniel realizes the dream is a picture of God's coming judgment on Nebuchadnezzar. He is honestly concerned for Nebuchadnezzar (and probably for himself). He knows that this king does not take bad news very well. Who knows what he will do to Daniel if Daniel speaks the truth?

When the king asks Daniel to give him the dream's meaning, he tells him not to sugar-coat the message, no matter how bad it might be. Nebuchadnezzar is not far enough along spiritually to act on the truth (that would take more time and a lot of suffering), but when that day came, he would know what he needed to do because of what Daniel told him. Daniel took a risk because he cared about Nebuchadnezzar. We all need people in our lives who love us enough to do this.

Questions 8–9

Jesus modeled how to handle interruptions. Indeed, an overview of the Gospels shows that Jesus' whole ministry looked like a series of interruptions. While at a dinner, he was interrupted by a sinful woman who began weeping at his feet. Trying to leave Jericho, he was interrupted by a blind man who wouldn't stop shouting his name. About to speak to a crowd, he was interrupted by a man who wanted him to perform a healing. While responding to that interruption, he encountered a woman who had been sick for over a decade and desired healing—an interruption within an interruption. Jesus was interrupted by lepers, children, religious leaders, sick people, and just about everyone else. Yet over and over he showed patience, grace, and love. Because he loved people so much, interruptions didn't seem like interruptions at all.

While Jesus was hanging on the cross dying for our sins, someone dared to ask him for a favor: "Remember me when you come into your kingdom." Even then, with nails though his hands and feet, Jesus did not seem to mind. He offered grace!

Questions 10–11

The reason God opposes pride so deeply is *not* that he is easily threatened by high achievers or obsessed with getting credit for everything or because it makes him feel better to watch us cringe. God opposes pride because it destroys us—the people that he loves — and it is radically antithetical to the good life he wants us to experience.

There is hope in humility. When we grow humble and resist pride, we look more like our heavenly Father. The greatest expression of humility and deference in all time and space is practiced in the fellowship of the Trinity. God is the humblest being in the universe. That is why God became flesh and walked among us. The incarnation was the most authentically humble action in all history. Not only did God come, but he served. Jesus even washed the dirty feet of sinful people, Judas included! Then God went to the cross to take our place, our sin, and our punishment. If we want to see the enduring hope that comes though humility, we need to look no further than Jesus.

Session Five — The Cost of Character
DANIEL 6

Question 1

In most cases, children's Bible storybooks are simplified for the purpose of being "age appropriate." There is no intention of changing the meaning of the text. Instead, the goal is to give kids a basic introduction to the story of Scripture in a way they can remember it. But, with time, we need to help people go deeper. There are rich, textured, and layered messages in the biblical narrative. As we mature physically, intellectually, and spiritually, God wants us to move past a preschool understanding to a deep encounter with him through the Word.

Questions 2–3

It is interesting to note how Daniel had stayed true to his convictions over the decades. A man of integrity and character, he had risen to places of significant leadership without compromising on the core issues of his faith. As his colleagues scoured his life looking for a place they could attack him, they came away shocked to discover:

- his conduct was exemplary,
- he showed no evidence of public or private corruption,
- he was trustworthy in his dealings,
- and, there was no sign of negligence in his work.

What a witness we would have in our world if we could just live with godly and biblical character.

At the end of the day, Daniel's fellow administrators determined that if they were going to trap him or trip him up, it would have to be something related to his faith.

One item often gets missed in this whole narrative. When the administrators came to Darius and suggested this grand idea of having the whole population pray only to him for thirty days, they told him that *all* of the leaders had agreed on this plan (Daniel 6:7). This was a lie. They had intentionally kept this information from Daniel. They were digging the hole and carefully placing twigs and leaves over it ... hoping Daniel would fall in.

A close study of this chapter also shows that Darius cared about Daniel, respected him, and did not want to see him executed. When Darius realized that he had been tricked, and was bound by his own edict, he was distressed. He did all he could to find a loophole, but there was none. When Daniel made it safely through the night, Darius was delighted ... and furious with those who had tried to have him killed.

By the end of the story Darius was praising Daniel's God. He also wrote a letter that he had distributed all over the kingdom. This letter gave praise and honor to God, and elevated Daniel even more. The letter and declaration of praise shows a very developed and healthy theology. God was at work in Darius.

Questions 4–6

We live at a time of human history when the basic ideas of right and wrong are under attack. People argue that truth is subjective and that we should all be able to embrace our own personal version of it. If we buy into this system of thought — and some Christ followers are dabbling on the edge — then the idea of character that reflects God's desire for us becomes very fluid. It used to be that people understood what words like *honesty*, *faithfulness*, and *purity* meant. Today there is a sense that these words mean whatever we want them to mean. The movement away from "God's truth" to "my truth" is changing everything.

Questions 7–8

All kinds of spiritual disciplines can strengthen our life of faith. For Daniel, prayer was one that he exercised with deep personal passion and conviction. If you want to go deeper into discovering and exercising the beauty of Christian disciplines, read Richard Foster's classic *Celebration of Discipline*. He talks about:

- *The Inward Disciplines:* Meditation, Prayer, Fasting, and Study
- *The Outward Disciplines:* Simplicity, Solitude, Submission, and Service
- *The Corporate Disciplines:* Confession, Worship, Guidance, and Celebration

Often we focus our energy and time on the disciplines of prayer and study of the Word, which of course are very important. But expanding to some of the other disciplines can bring life and freshness to our faith.

Questions 9–11

A beautiful partnership existed between Daniel's life of character and his verbal witness. He walked the walk, but he also talked the talk. When King Darius came to the lions' den to see if Daniel had made it safely through the night, Daniel let him know that God had protected him by sending an angel to shut the mouths of the lions. By the way, the lions were very hungry, as evidenced by how they responded when their next meal was dropped into the den!

Today it is very popular to talk about being a witness without using words. Daniel's life tells another story. It is a picture of a life that gives witness *and* words that reinforce the message of his life. We could all learn from this kind of a balanced approach.

Session Six – Dreams and Visions
DANIEL 7:1–14

Question 1–2

When reading apocalyptic literature, you must always start with the context and begin by asking what the writer intends his readers to understand. Daniel is writing to the people of God in exile during the first year of Belshazzar, king of Babylon. In other words, Nebuchadnezzar, who had been converted, who was following God—which must have brought hope to the people of Israel—is now dead. The people are living under a new king who is quite twisted. In Daniel 7, we find words of hope to people who are in what looks like a hopeless situation.

Unfortunately, many people down through the centuries of church history have tried to turn these apocalyptic passages into a key for understanding exactly what is happening in current political and economic times. They look at the beasts and the images in this chapter and use them to play prophetic guessing games.

At various points in history people have guessed that the ten horns stood for ten kings in the Greek Empire, for kings set up by Napoleon, for NATO, and for nations in the European Common Market, just to name a few. The problem with this approach is you can go around looking for any organization with ten members and think you have Daniel all figured out.

I believe this is a wrong approach to interpreting Scripture. Every time people are wrong (and they have been very wrong lots of times), the gospel loses credibility with a watching world.

Questions 3–5

In a day of prosperity teachers in the church and countless products being produced each year to make our lives more comfortable, it is not good news to hear that suffering is part of our faith. But, think about it for a moment—many of the great people of faith from Bible days to the present have faced persecution, suffering, and struggles.

The apostle Paul wrote, "Everyone who wants to live a godly life in Christ Jesus will be persecuted" (2 Timothy 3:12). The apostle Peter wrote, "Dear friends, do not be surprised at the painful trial you are suffering, as though something strange were happening to you. But rejoice that you participate in the sufferings of Christ, so that you may be overjoyed when his glory is revealed" (1 Peter 4:12–13). Jesus showed us the way to live and he ended up on a cross. Paul and Peter died martyrs' deaths. Who are we to think that we should glide through life without scars and struggles?

Midway through Daniel's vision (verse 9) there is an abrupt change in scenery. For as long as people have walked the earth they've asked: What is God like? Who is he really? Daniel begins using symbols and imagery to answer those very questions.

First, Daniel makes it clear that God is just and brings justice. Daniel says, "Thrones were set in place and God took his seat." This is not just about seating arrangements. Daniel is saying that God is going to set things right.

Many horrible things happen in this world. We watch them on the news each evening and we shake our heads. We wonder, "Can this world ever be redeemed? Will there ever be justice?" One day God will bring it to pass. The Ancient of Days is going to take his seat. There is a throne, and it will be occupied. God is going to set things right. We need to remember that Daniel knew all about injustice. He had been captured and exiled by one king, discarded by another, thrown into a lions' den by a third. He had suffered deep pain from people in seats of power. He must have wondered, "Will justice ever be served?" God says, "The day is coming. There is a throne."

Second, Daniel assures us that God is pure and holy. The picture of God's clothing and hair being white as snow and white like wool is a vision of purity. This is a common image in Scripture. Isaiah says, "Though your sins be as scarlet, they shall be as white as snow."

God is perfectly holy. He is utterly pure. Through all eternity he has never done a thing, spoken a word, or entertained a thought that was anything less than honorable, true, beautiful, and good. Jesus said, "Blessed are the pure in heart, for they shall see God." First John 3:3 says, "Everyone who has this hope" — this hope in the returning Christ, this hope that God will set things right one day — "purifies himself, just as he is pure."

Third, the images of fire and flame point to God's power. Remember the burning bush that was not consumed, the pillar of fire that delivered the Israelites from Pharaoh, the fire from heaven that Elijah called down to consume an offering, and the tongues of fire that revealed the presence and power of the Holy

Spirit at Pentecost. God is more powerful than we can dream or imagine.

Question 10

The God we worship, the Ancient of Days, is an infinite God. His power is not challenged by any force in the universe. God allows the spiritual struggle in this world to go on because his desire is that people should freely choose to turn to him. This is exactly why Peter writes in 2 Peter 3:9, "The Lord is not slow in keeping his promise"—his promise to return—"as some understand slowness. He is patient with you, not wanting anyone to perish, but everyone to come to repentance."

We live in the day of God's patience, and so this fallen world goes on. But don't be fooled. Once he decides that the struggle is over, once he decides that the opportunity for decision is done and the time for judgment has come, he is not going to need a long time and lots of firepower to win that final battle. He holds all power. Satan himself could not exist a second if it were not for the sustaining power of God. When God says it's over, it will be over.

We value your thoughts about what you've just read.
Please share them with us. You'll find contact information
in the back of this book.

WILLOW
Willow Creek Association

Willow Creek Association
Vision, Training, Resources for Prevailing Churches

This resource was created to serve you and to help you build a local church that prevails. It is just one of many ministry tools that are part of the Willow Creek Resources® line, published by the Willow Creek Association together with Zondervan.

The Willow Creek Association (WCA) was created in 1992 to serve a rapidly growing number of churches from across the denominational spectrum that are committed to helping unchurched people become fully devoted followers of Christ. Membership in the WCA now numbers over 12,000 Member Churches worldwide from more than ninety denominations.

The Willow Creek Association links like-minded Christian leaders with each other and with strategic vision, training, and resources in order to help them build prevailing churches designed to reach their redemptive potential. Here are some of the ways the WCA does that.

- **The Leadership Summit**—a once a year, two-and-a-half-day conference to envision and equip Christians with leadership gifts and responsibilities. Presented live at Willow Creek as well as via satellite broadcast to over 130 locations across North America, this event is designed to increase the leadership effectiveness of pastors, ministry staff, volunteer church leaders, and Christians in the marketplace.

- **Ministry-Specific Conferences**—throughout each year the WCA hosts a variety of conferences and training events—both at Willow Creek's main campus and offsite, across the U.S., and around the world—targeting church leaders and volunteers in ministry-specific areas such as: small groups, preaching and teaching, the arts, children, students, volunteers, stewardship, etc.

- **Willow Creek Resources**®—provides churches with trusted and field-tested ministry resources in such areas as leadership, evangelism, spiritual formation, spiritual gifts, small groups, stewardship, student ministry, children's ministry, the use of the arts—drama, media, contemporary music—and more.

- **WCA Member Benefits**—includes substantial discounts to WCA training events, a 20 percent discount on all Willow Creek Resources®, *Defining Moments* monthly audio journal for leaders, quarterly *Willow* magazine, access to a Members-Only section on WillowNet, monthly communications, and more. Member Churches also receive special discounts and premier services through WCA's growing number of ministry partners—Select Service Providers—and save an average of $500 annually depending on the level of engagement.

For specific information about WCA conferences, resources, membership, and other ministry services contact:

Willow Creek Association
P.O. Box 3188
Barrington, IL 60011-3188
Phone: 847-570-9812
Fax: 847-765-5046
www.willowcreek.com

Just Walk Across the Room Curriculum Kit

Simple Steps Pointing People to Faith

Bill Hybels with *Ashley Wiersma*

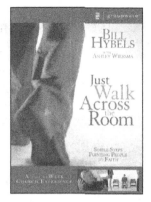

In *Just Walk Across the Room*, Bill Hybels brings personal evangelism into the twenty-first century with a natural and empowering approach modeled after Jesus himself. When Christ "walked" clear across the cosmos more than 2,000 years ago, he had no forced formulas and no memorized script; rather, he came armed only with an offer of redemption for people like us, many of whom were neck-deep in pain of their own making.

This dynamic four-week experience is designed to equip and inspire your entire church to participate in that same pattern of grace-giving by taking simple walks across rooms—leaving your circles of comfort and extending hands of care, compassion, and inclusiveness to people who might need a touch of God's love today.

Expanding on the principles set forth in Hybels' book of the same name, *Just Walk Across the Room* consists of three integrated components:

- Sermons, an implementation guide, and church promotional materials provided on CD-ROM to address the church as a whole
- Small group DVD and a participant's guide to enable people to work through the material in small, connected circles of community
- The book *Just Walk Across the Room* to allow participants to think through the concepts individually

Mixed Media Set: 978-0-310-27172-7

Pick up a copy at your favorite bookstore!

When the Game Is Over, It All Goes Back in the Box DVD

Six Sessions on Living Life in the Light of Eternity

John Ortberg with *Stephen* and
Amanda Sorenson

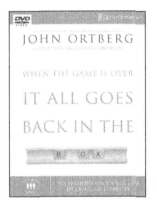

Using his humor and his genius for storytelling, John Ortberg helps you focus on the real rules of the game of life and how to set your priorities. *When the Game Is Over, It All Goes Back in the Box DVD* and participant's guide help explain how, left to our own devices, we tend to seek out worldly things, mistakenly thinking they will bring us fulfillment. But everything on Earth belongs to God. Everything we "own" is just on loan. And what pleases God is often 180 degrees from what we may think is important.

In the six sessions you will learn how to:

- Live passionately and boldly
- Learn how to be active players in the game that pleases God
- Find your true mission and offer your best
- Fill each square on the board with what matters most
- Seek the richness of being instead of the richness of having

You can't beat the house, notes Ortberg. We're playing our game of life on a giant board called a calendar. Time will always run out, so it's a good thing to live a life that delights your Creator. When everything goes back in the box, you'll have made what is temporary a servant to what is eternal, and you'll leave this life knowing you've achieved the only victory that matters.

This DVD includes a 32-page leader's guide and is designed to be used with the *When the Game Is Over, It All Goes Back in the Box* participant's guide, which is available separately.

DVD-ROM: 978-0-310-28247-1
Participant's Guide: 978-0-310-28246-4

Pick up a copy at your favorite bookstore!

The Case for Christ DVD

A Six-Session Investigation of the Evidence for Jesus

Lee Strobel and *Garry Poole*

Is there credible evidence that Jesus of Nazareth really is the Son of God?

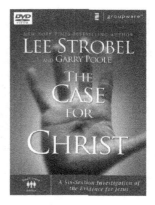

Retracing his own spiritual journey from atheism to faith, Lee Strobel, former legal editor of the *Chicago Tribune*, cross-examines several experts with doctorates from schools like Cambridge, Princeton, and Brandeis who are recognized authorities in their own fields.

Strobel challenges them with questions like:

- How reliable is the New Testament?
- Does evidence for Jesus exist outside the Bible?
- Is there any reason to believe the resurrection was an actual event?

Strobel's tough, point-blank questions make this six-session video study a captivating, fast-paced experience. But it's not fiction. It's a riveting quest for the truth about history's most compelling figure.

The six sessions include:

1. The Investigation of a Lifetime
2. Eyewitness Evidence
3. Evidence Outside the Bible
4. Analyzing Jesus
5. Evidence for the Resurrection
6. Reaching the Verdict

6 sessions; 1 DVD with leader's guide, 80 minutes (approximate). *The Case for Christ* participant's guide is available separately.

DVD-ROM: 978-0-310-28280-8
Participant's Guide: 978-0-310-28282-2

The Case for a Creator DVD

A Six-Session Investigation of the Scientific Evidence That Points toward God

Lee Strobel and *Garry Poole*

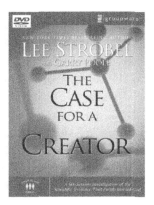

Former journalist and skeptic Lee Strobel has discovered something very interesting about science. Far from being the enemy of faith, science may now provide a solid foundation for believing in God.

Has science finally discovered God? Certainly new discoveries in such scientific disciplines as cosmology, cellular biology, astronomy, physics and DNA research are pointing to the incredible complexity of our universe, a complexity best explained by the existence of a Creator.

Written by Lee Strobel and Garry Poole, this six-session, 80-minute DVD curriculum comes with a companion participant's guide along with a leader's guide. The kit is based on Strobel's book and documentary *The Case for a Creator* and invites participants to encounter a diverse and impressive body of new scientific research that supports the belief in God. Weighty and complex evidence is delivered in a compelling conversational style.

The six sessions include:

1. Science and God
2. Doubts about Darwinism
3. The Evidence of Cosmology
4. The Fine-tuning of the Universe
5. The Evidence of Biochemistry
6. DNA and the Origin of Life

The Case for a Creator participant's guide is available separately.

DVD-ROM: 978-0-310-28283-9
Participant's Guide: 978-0-310-28285-3

The Case for Faith DVD

A Six-Session Investigation of the Toughest Objections to Christianity

Lee Strobel and *Garry Poole*

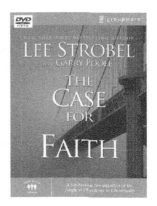

Doubt is familiar territory for Lee Strobel, the former atheist and award-winning author of books for skeptics and Christians. But he believes that faith and reason go hand in hand, and that Christianity is a defensible religion.

In this six-session video curriculum, Strobel uses his journalistic approach to explore the most common emotional obstacles to faith in Christ. These include the natural inclination to wrestle with faith and doubt, the troubling presence of evil and suffering in the world, and the exclusivity of the Christian gospel. They also include this compelling question: Can I doubt and be a Christian?

Through compelling video of personal stories and experts addressing these topics, combined with reflection and interaction, Christians and spiritual seekers will learn how to overcome these obstacles, deepen their spiritual convictions, and find new confidence that Christianity is a reasonable faith.

The Case for Faith participant's guide is available separately.

DVD-ROM: 978-0-310-24116-4
Participant's Guide: 978-0-310-24114-0

Pick up a copy at your favorite bookstore!

ReGroup™

Training Groups to Be Groups

Henry Cloud, Bill Donahue, and *John Townsend*

Whether you're a new or seasoned group leader, or whether your group is well-established or just getting started, the *ReGroup™* small group DVD and participant's guide will lead you and your group together to a remarkable new closeness and effectiveness. Designed to foster healthy group interaction and facilitate maximum growth, this innovative approach equips both group leaders and members with essential skills and values for creating and sustaining truly life-changing small groups. Created by three group life experts, the two DVDs in this kit include:

- Four sixty-minute sessions on the foundations of small groups that include teaching by the authors, creative segments, and activities and discussion time
- Thirteen five-minute coaching segments on topics such as active listening, personal sharing, giving and receiving feedback, prayer, calling out the best in others, and more

A participant's guide is sold separately.

DVD: 978-0-310-27783-5
Participant's Guide: 978-0-310-27785-9

Pick up a copy at your favorite bookstore!

ZONDERVAN®
.com

No Perfect People Allowed
(with 4-Week Church Experience DVD)

Creating a Come as You Are Culture in the Church

John Burke

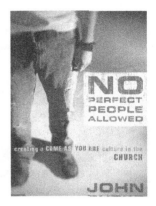

How do we live out the message of Jesus in today's ever-changing culture?

The church is facing its greatest challenge—and its greatest opportunity—in our postmodern, post-Christian world. God is drawing thousands of spiritually curious "imperfect people" to become his church—but how are we doing at welcoming them?

No Perfect People Allowed shows you how to deconstruct the five main barriers standing between emerging generations and your church by creating the right culture. From inspiring stories of real people once far from God, to practical ideas that can be applied by any local church, this book offers a refreshing vision of the potential and power of the body of Christ to transform lives today.

"We now are living in a post-Christian America—and that means we must be rethinking ministry through a missionary mindset. What makes this book both unique and extremely helpful is that it is filled with real-life stories of post-Christian people becoming followers of Jesus—not just statistics or data about them."

Dan Kimball, Author, *The Emerging Church*

"... John's 'get it' factor with people, lost or found, is something to behold! Reading this book filled me with optimism regarding the next generation of pastors and faith communities ..."

Bill Hybels, Senior Pastor, Willow Creek Community Church

"*No Perfect People Allowed* is a timely and necessary word for church leaders in a post-Christian culture. John Burke serves up quite a tasty meal full of the rich nutrients that will strengthen the body of Christ."

Randy Frazee, Senior Minister, Oak Hills Church;
Author, *The Connecting Church* and *Making Room for Life*

Hardcover, Jacketed: 978-0-310-27807-8